Looking at
MEXICO

Kathleen Pohl

Gareth Stevens
Publishing

WITHDRAWN

FREMONT PUBLIC LIBRARY DISTRICT
1170 N. Midlothian Road
Mundelein, IL 60060

Please visit our web site at: www.garethstevens.com
For a free color catalog describing our list of high-quality books,
call 1-800-542-2595 (USA) or 1-800-387-3178 (Canada).

Library of Congress Cataloging-in-Publication Data

Pohl, Kathleen.
    Looking at Mexico / Kathleen Pohl. — North American ed.
        p. cm. — (Looking at countries)
    Includes index.
    ISBN: 978-0-8368-8172-1 (lib. bdg.)
    ISBN: 978-0-8368-8179-0 (softcover)
    1. Mexico—Juvenile literature. I. Title.
    F1208.5.P64   2008
    972—dc22   2007003004

This edition first published in 2008 by
Gareth Stevens Publishing
A Weekly Reader® Company
1 Reader's Digest Road
Pleasantville, NY 10570-7000 USA

Managing editor: Valerie J. Weber
Editor: Gini Holland
Art direction: Tammy West
Graphic designer: Dave Kowalski
Photo research: Diane Laska-Swanke
Production: Jessica Yanke

Photo credits: (t=top, b=bottom, l=left, r=right, c=center)
© Larry Dunmire/DDB Stock Photo: cover; © John Neubauer/PhotoEdit: 1, 8, 12, 17t, 20;
Dave Kowalski/© Gareth Stevens, Inc.: 4, 5t, 31; © Chris Sharp/DDB Stock Photo: 5b, 6, 15t;
© Byron Augustin/DDB Stock Photo: 7; © H. Huntly Hersch/DDB Stock Photo: 9; © Carver
Mostardi/DDB Stock Photo: 10, 13t; © Suzanne Murphy-Larronde/DDB Stock Photo: 11t, 19b;
© Bruce Herman/DDB Stock Photo: 11b; © Carlos Pereyra/DDB Stock Photo: 13b; © Bonnie
Kamin/PhotoEdit: 14; © Carla del Mar/DDB Stock Photo: 15b; © J. P. Courau/DDB Stock Photo:
16, 25t; © Paul Conklin/PhotoEdit: 17b; © D. Donne Bryant/DDB Stock Photo: 18, 19t, 27b;
© Jeff Greenberg/PhotoEdit: 21t; © Stewart Aitchison/DDB Stock Photo: 21b; © Vince
DeWitt/DDB Stock Photo: 22; © Simon Scoones/EASI-Images/CFW Images: 23t; © Spencer
Grant/PhotoEdit: 23b, 24; © Craig Raney/DDB Stock Photo: 25b; © Rudi Von Briel/PhotoEdit: 26;
© John Cotter/DDB Stock Photo: 27t; © Diane Laska-Swanke: 27c

Printed in the United States of America

1 2 3 4 5 6 7 8 9 11 10 09 08 07

Contents

Words that appear in the glossary are printed in **boldface** type the first time they occur in the text.

Where Is Mexico?

Mexico shares the continent of North America with the United States and Canada. It lies to the south of the United States and north of Guatemala and Belize. Water surrounds much of Mexico. The Gulf of Mexico and the Caribbean Sea lie on Mexico's eastern coast. The Pacific Ocean is on the western coast.

The country's capital is Mexico City. It lies in a valley on Mexico's central high plain, or **plateau**. The city is huge, crowded, and full of busy streets, shops, restaurants, businesses, and landmarks. The ancient ruin of Teotihuacán is nearby.

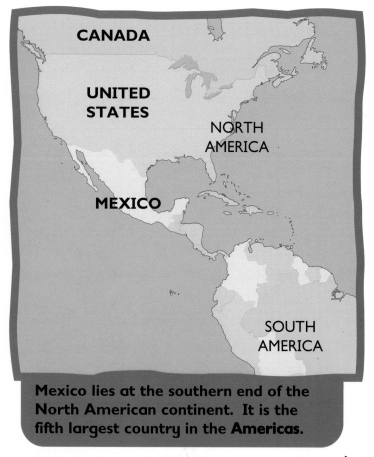

Mexico lies at the southern end of the North American continent. It is the fifth largest country in the **Americas**.

Did you know?

The Rio Grande, which means "Big River," forms two-thirds of the border between Mexico and the United States.

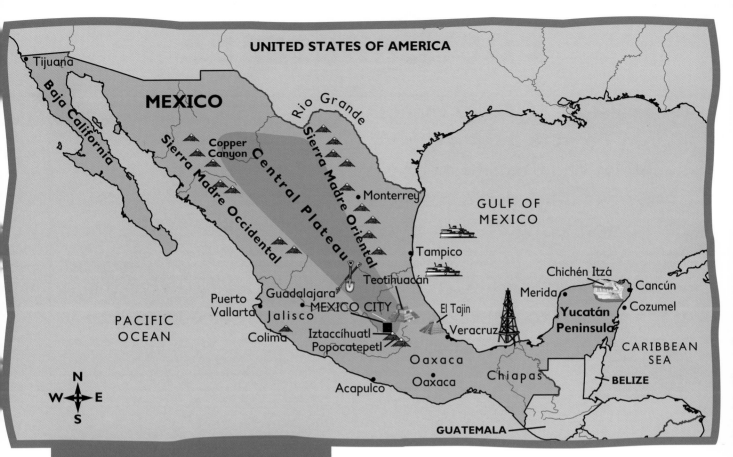

This map shows all the places that are mentioned in this book.

Mexico's two **peninsulas** are Baja California in the northwest and the Yucatan Peninsula in the southeast. Mexico also has tiny islands off of both coasts. Two of its most popular island **resorts** are Canún and Cozumel in the Caribbean Sea.

People enjoy walking and eating lunch in the Plaza de Armas in Mérida, Yucatán.

5

The Landscape

The landscape of Mexico changes a lot from north to south and from its mountains and plains to its coasts. Cactus and other desert plants dot the dry northern part. Jungles and rain forests grow in the south. Beautiful sandy beaches, such as the popular tourist area of Puerto Vallarta, line Mexico's coasts.

The cardon cactus, which lives in the desert in Baja California, is the world's largest cactus! It can grow as tall as a six-story building.

Mexico's Copper Canyon is deeper and covers a larger area than the Grand Canyon in the United States! It lies in the Sierra Madre Occidental Mountains.

In the middle of Mexico lies a high plain called the Central Plateau, where most Mexicans live. The Sierra Madre Mountains tower along the sides of the plateau. The eastern mountains are called Oriental and the western mountains are called Occidental.

Mexico is a land of volcanoes — and sometimes earthquakes! Two volcanoes that are still active are Colima, south of the city of Guadalajara, and Popocatepetl, near Mexico City. The name Popocatepetl comes from the Aztec Indian word meaning "smoking mountain."

Weather and Seasons

Mexico's mild climate and sunny weather make it a favorite place for tourists. Even though the country is warm, some mountains in Mexico have peaks covered with snow year-round. Mexico does not have all four seasons of spring, summer, winter, and fall. Instead, Mexico has only two seasons, rainy and dry. In some areas, even the rainy season is quite dry.

Did you know?

From June through September, strong storms and **hurricanes** sometimes form along Mexico's coasts.

Tall hotels line the sandy beach at Acapulco, Mexico, a popular tourist resort.

Iztaccíhuatl and Popocatepetl are two volcanoes near Mexico City. "Popo," shown smoking here, sometimes spits ash as well as smoke into the sky!

The amount of rainfall varies a lot from north to south. Northern Mexico is very dry, with hot "summers" and cool "winters." Central Mexico is also dry, with mild weather year-round. Much more rain falls in southern Mexico along the coast and on the Yucatán Peninsula. The air is hot and **humid** in this **tropical** part of Mexico.

Did you know?

The average temperature along the coast of Mexico is 77 °F (25 °C). In the mountains, it is a pleasant 63 °F (17 °C).

Mexican People

About 105 million people live in Mexico. It is the largest Spanish-speaking country in the world. Today, Mexico blends the **cultures** of the Indian groups who have always lived there and the Spanish who ruled the country for three hundred years.

Religion has always been important in Mexico. The Aztec and Mayan Indian tribes once built great stone **temples**. Some of these are still standing. Today, most people in Mexico are Roman Catholics, and a few are Protestants or Jews. Still others follow the ancient Indian religions.

On December 12, people throughout Mexico celebrate the Day of Our Lady of Guadalupe, the patron saint of all Mexicans.

Did you know?

A **fiesta** is held each year to honor the **patron saint**, or "protector," of each village, city, and state in Mexico. These celebrations are called saint's days.

Mexico's famous street musicians perform at the Mariachi Festival held every September in the city of Guadalajara.

Ancient stone temples built by the Mayan Indians still stand at Chichén Itzá in Yucatán.

Many Mexican holidays, or fiestas, celebrate religious events. On these days, many people dress in colorful outfits, watch fireworks and parades, and listen to **mariachi bands**.

Mexico has thirty-one states. Each state has its own capital city and state government. Each state has its own **traditions**, or styles of dress, music, and dance.

School and Family

Children in Mexico must go to school from ages six to fourteen. Because schools are crowded, most students go to elementary school for only four hours a day. Some go in the morning, while others attend in the afternoon. They go to elementary school for six years and middle school for three years. After that, some students begin working, while others continue their education in high school and college.

Students in Mexico usually wear school uniforms. They study Spanish, math, science, history, geography, art, and music.

All eyes are on the teacher in this elementary school classroom in Acapulco.

Tortillas (*in the big serving bowl*) are on the table more often than bread when Mexican families sit down to eat.

Soccer, called *futbol*, is a popular sport in Mexico. These children are playing on a soccer field at a college in Mexico City.

Family ties are strong in Mexico. Children, parents, and grand-parents often live together. On Sunday, many families go to church. After church, they sit down to a *comida*, the midday meal. Families celebrate birthdays and saint's days together.

Country Life

About one out of every four people in Mexico lives on a farm or in a small village. Steep mountains and dry weather make it hard to farm in most of Mexico. The best farmland is at the southern end of the Central Plateau and in the hot, rainy south. In the dry north, ranchers raise cattle.

In many rural areas of Mexico, families use the local bus to travel from one village to another.

In very poor areas in Mexico, farmers still use burros to gather fruits and vegetables and take them to market.

A young girl sells pottery in Oaxaca, an area known for its handmade crafts.

Mexico has some large, modern farms. Most of its farms, however, are small and poor. Some farmers use small donkeys called burros to take their fruits and vegetables to nearby villages to sell. Farm children help with chores. They often look after chickens and goats. Farmers and their families work hard, but most are very poor.

Mexico's main crops include corn, coffee, beans, cotton, sugarcane, bananas, wheat, and vanilla. Mexicans also grow cacao, the plant from which chocolate is made. Many people in rural Mexico also make crafts to sell to tourists.

15

City Life

Since the 1950s, Mexico's cities have grown quickly. Mexico City and its **suburbs** now have more than eighteen million people. It is the second largest city in the world! Only Tokyo, Japan, has more people. Mexico City's streets are noisy and crowded with traffic jams. Air pollution is also a major problem.

Mexico City has an international airport, a modern subway, and a public bus system. This city is home to Mexico's government buildings and the largest church in the country. It also has factories, banks, shops, tall office buildings, museums, and beautiful parks.

People enjoy relaxing in Chapultepec Park, Mexico City's largest park.

A huge crowd gathers around the flag to celebrate Columbus Day, October 12, at the Zocalo Plaza in Mexico City.

Many poor people live in crowded housing in the **slums** outside of Mexico City.

Mexico City also contains a historic town square called the Zocalo. In cities and villages in Mexico, the town square is the center of social life. People often walk in the town squares to meet friends and listen to music.

Did you know?

Mexico City is built on the site of the ancient Aztec city of Tenochtitlán, making it the oldest city in the Americas!

Mexican Houses

One of Mexico's oldest building materials is adobe, or sun-dried clay. Houses made of white adobe with red tile roofs can be seen throughout the country.

In Mexico's cities, many people live in modern, tall apartment buildings. Some wealthy people live in beautiful homes that are built around courtyards. Tall trees and lush flowers usually fill the courtyards.

Some people in Mexico City live in modern apartment buildings with plenty of parking space.

Some of Mexico City's poorest people live in Neza Village, a neighborhood of crowded shacks near the city dump.

Middle-class homes line the streets of this town near Veracruz.

The poorer areas of the city are called slums. Here, many people crowd into tiny metal houses or cardboard shacks. In rural areas, people often live in one-room huts made out of sticks and mud and covered with **thatched** roofs.

Did you know?

Many homes in Mexico's city slums and countryside have no running water or electricity.

Mexican Food

Customers shop for fresh vegetables and fruits at an outdoor market in Oaxaca.

Many people in Mexico like spicy foods. They add chili peppers to spice up many dishes. Corn, beans, tomatoes, rice, and peppers are common in Mexican foods.

Did you know?

Made from spices, dried peppers, and chocolate, mole is a popular sauce for meat. It is served over chicken.

People in rural areas often eat tortillas and frijoles with every meal. Tortillas are flat, round breads made of cornmeal or flour. Frijoles are red or black beans that are boiled, mashed, fried, and refried. A popular dessert throughout Mexico, flan is a custard-like pudding. Made from sugar and eggs, it tastes like caramel.

A Zapotec Indian mother and her daughter cook tortillas over a fire in the southern state of Oaxaca.

People in Mexico often shop in outdoor markets for fresh fruits, vegetables, chicken, and fish. They also go to grocery stores, bakeries, cafés, and restaurants.

Popular Mexican foods include tamales, enchiladas, frijoles, hot chile peppers, and salsa.

At Work

Many people in Mexico work in restaurants and hotels and as store clerks and teachers. Many others work in the booming tourist trade in resort towns along the coasts. Others make beautiful pottery, silver jewelry, colorful blankets, and weavings to sell to tourists.

Mexico's factories produce everything from paper and clothing to chemicals, cars, and car parts. The city of Monterrey in northeast Mexico has big factories and iron and steel **foundries**. Mexico's largest **seaports** are Veracruz and Tampico on the Gulf of Mexico.

Mexico City has elegant restaurants where chefs prepare fancy meals.

Women in the villages of Chiapas weave clothing on back-strap looms. Each village is known for its own style of weaving and clothing.

In a factory in Tijuana, workers put together electronic parts.

Mexico leads the world in silver production. Other minerals found in Mexico include copper, gold, lead, salt, and zinc. Its oil wells pump enough oil for Mexico to use and sell to other countries.

Did you know?

The first Coca-Cola bottling plant in Mexico was built in Tampico in 1926.

Having Fun

Many Mexicans of all ages like soccer and baseball, Mexico's most popular sports. Mexico has professional baseball and soccer teams. Boxing, horse racing, and bullfighting are popular **spectator sports**.

Most young people like to listen to Mexico's pop stars on the radio. Some like to dance at discos. Many enjoy watching television and going to the movies.

Did you know?

The World Cup soccer finals have been held several times at the Aztec Stadium in Mexico City.

A huge Christmas **piñata** floats in front of the cathedral in the Zocalo Plaza in Mexico City.

Colorfully dressed dancers from the state of Jalisco perform a traditional folk dance in Mexico City.

People like to swim and relax at Mexico's beautiful beaches. Many Mexicans like to explore art and history museums and historic ruins and go to concerts and dances. The Ballet Folklorico in Mexico City is the most famous dance company in Mexico. This company brings the dances of old Mexico to life for all to enjoy.

A matador waves his cape during a bullfight in Baja California.

Mexico: The Facts

- Spanish is the main language of Mexico. Many Indian languages are also spoken in different parts of Mexico.

- The full name for Mexico is Estados Unidos Mexicanos (United Mexican States). Mexico is a **federal republic**. The president, who serves one six-year term, heads the government.

- Mexico is divided into thirty-one states and one federal district. Mexico City and its southern suburbs make up the federal district, which is the center of national government.

- Citizens of Mexico who are eighteen years old or older may vote in the country's elections.

The flag of Mexico has color bars of green, white, and red. In the center of the white bar is Mexico's **coat of arms**. It is an image of an eagle with a snake in its mouth. This symbol is from an ancient Aztec legend.

The Mexican currency is based on the peso. There are 100 centavos, or cents, in one peso. Both paper money and coins are used in Mexico.

Did you know?

Mexico is about one-fifth the size of the United States.

Many tourists visit Mexico's ancient Indian ruins each year. The Pyramid of the Niches in El Tajin, Veracruz, has 365 openings — one for each day of the year!

Glossary

Americas – the areas of North, South, and Central America

coat of arms – a special symbol that stands for a particular family or country

cultures – specific groups or nations of people that share the same basic backgrounds and beliefs within each group

federal republic – a country where the central government has only limited power and in which states have some self-government

fiesta – festival or time of celebration

foundries – buildings where metals are melted and made into different shapes

highlands – mountainous lands

humid – having a lot of moisture in the air, which can make the air feel heavy and sticky

hurricanes – fierce storms that sometimes form over the ocean. Their strong winds and heavy rains can cause great damage to land, plants, and buildings.

mariachi bands – groups of colorfully costumed musicians who stroll in the streets as they perform

patron saint – a holy or godly person whose spirit is believed to protect a person or place

peninsulas – strips of land that are surrounded by water on three sides

piñata – a candy-filled paper shape made for a holiday game

plateau – a high plain

resorts – places, often near lakes or oceans, that have food, lodging, and entertainment for visitors who come there for vacations

seaports – towns or cities near the sea where goods are shipped out or brought in

spectator sports – sports that large groups of people watch on television, in sports stadiums, or in other arenas

slums – very poor, run-down neighborhoods

suburbs – communities next to or near larger cities

temples – buildings made by people who practice a religion to honor God or gods and goddesses

thatched – made of straw, often for a roof of a house

traditions – a people's way of living and beliefs that have been passed down through many years

tropical – having a hot and steamy climate where rainfall is plentiful

volcanoes – mountains that are formed when lava and ash explode through Earth's crust. The lava comes from Earth's hot, liquid center.

Find Out More

Mexico for Kids
www.elbalero.gob.mx/index_kids.html

Pyramids of Mesoamerica
www.crystalinks.com/pyramidmesoamerica.html

Fast Facts for Kids
www.kidskonnect.com/Mexico/MexicoHome.html

Publisher's note to educators and parents: Our editors have carefully reviewed these Web sites to ensure that they are suitable for children. Many Web sites change frequently, however, and we cannot guarantee that a site's future contents will continue to meet our high standards of quality and educational value. Be advised that children should be closely supervised whenever they access the Internet.

My Map of Mexico

Photocopy or trace the map on page 31. Then write in the names of the countries, bodies of water, states, islands, cities and towns, and land areas, pyramids, and ruins listed below. (Look at the map on page 5 if you need help.) After you have written in the names of all the places, find some crayons and color the map!

Countries
Belize
Guatemala
Mexico
United States

Bodies of Water
Caribbean Sea
Gulf of Mexico
Pacific Ocean
Rio Grande

States
Chiapas
Jalisco
Oaxaca

Islands and Island Groups
Cancún
Cozumel

Cities and Towns
Acapulco
Guadalajara
Mérida

Mexico City
Monterrey
Oaxaca
Puerto Vallarta
Tampico
Tijuana
Veracruz

Land Areas, Mountains, and Volcanoes
Baja California
Central Plateau
Colima volcano
Copper Canyon
Iztaccíhuatl volcano
Popocatepetl volcano
Sierra Madre Occidental
Sierra Madre Oriental
Yucatán Peninsula

Pyramids and Ruins
Chichén Itzá
El Tajin
Teotihuacán

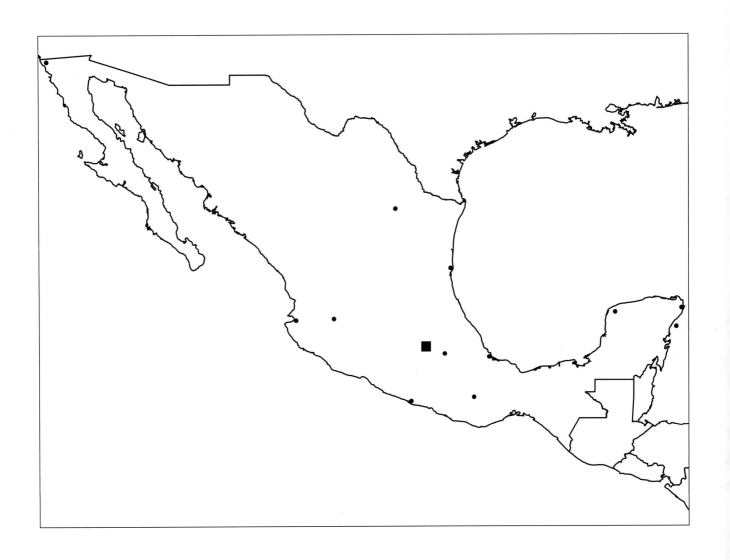

Index